20 best
baby shower
recipes

Houghton Mifflin Harcourt
Boston • New York • 2013

Copyright © 2013 by General Mills, Minneapolis, Minnesota. All rights reserved.

For information about permission to reproduce selections from this book, write to Permissions, Houghton Mifflin Harcourt Publishing Company, 215 Park Avenue South, New York, New York 10003.

www.hmhco.com

Cover photo: Baby Rattle Cupcakes (page 22)

General Mills
Food Content and Relationship Marketing Director: Geoff Johnson
Food Content Marketing Manager: Susan Klobuchar
Senior Editor: Grace Wells
Kitchen Manager: Ann Stuart
Recipe Development and Testing: Betty Crocker Kitchens
Photography: General Mills Photography Studios and Image Library

Houghton Mifflin Harcourt
Publisher: Natalie Chapman
Editorial Director: Cindy Kitchel
Executive Editor: Anne Ficklen
Associate Editor: Heather Dabah
Managing Editor: Rebecca Springer
Production Editor: Kristi Hart
Cover Design: Chrissy Kurpeski
Book Design: Tai Blanche

ISBN 978-0-544-31463-4
Printed in the United States of America

The Betty Crocker Kitchens seal guarantees success in your kitchen. Every recipe has been tested in America's Most Trusted Kitchens™ to meet our high standards of reliability, easy preparation and great taste.

FIND MORE GREAT IDEAS AT
BettyCrocker.com

Dear Friends,

This new collection of colorful mini books has been put together with you in mind because we know that you love great recipes and enjoy cooking and baking but have a busy lifestyle. So every little book in the series contains just 20 recipes for you to treasure and enjoy. Plus, each book is a single subject designed in a bite-size format just for you—it's easy to use and is filled with favorite recipes from the Betty Crocker Kitchens!

All of the books are conveniently divided into short chapters so you can quickly find what you're looking for, and the beautiful photos throughout are sure to entice you into making the delicious recipes. In the series, you'll discover a fabulous array of recipes to spark your interest—from cookies, cupcakes and birthday cakes to party ideas for a variety of occasions. There's grilled foods, potluck favorites and even gluten-free recipes too.

You'll love the variety in these mini books—so pick one or choose them all for your cooking pleasure.

Enjoy and happy cooking!

Sincerely,

Betty Crocker

contents

Savory Bites
Baby Bib Appetizers 6
Hummus and Cucumber Bites 7
Roasted Red Bell Pepper and Goat Cheese Bites 8
Mango-Pepper Salsa Crostini 9
Tomato-Artichoke Bruschetta with Feta 10
Fresh Mozzarella in Tomato Cups 11
Festive Fillo Crab Cups 12

Petite Treats
Baby Block Cereal Bars 13
Lemon Linzer Bars 14
Almond Petits Fours 15
Mini Almond-Butter Tea Cakes 16
Salted Caramel Turtle Triangles 17
Cherry-Topped Chocolate Tassies 18
Luscious Chocolate Truffles 19

Celebratory Cakes
Baby's Booties 20
Baby Rattle Cupcakes 22
Baby Face Cake 23
Baby Buggy Cake 24
Baby's Bib Cake 25
Baby Block Cake 26

Metric Conversion Guide 28
Recipe Testing and Calculating Nutrition Information 29

Savory Bites

Baby Bib Appetizers

Prep Time: 35 Minutes • **Start to Finish:** 35 Minutes • Makes 24 appetizers

24 slices (¾ oz each) Cheddar cheese

6 slices (1 oz each) oval-shaped deli cooked ham

½ cup garlic-and-herbs spreadable cheese (from 6.5-oz container)

24 slices cocktail rye bread (from 1-lb package)

24 long, thin fresh chives

Fresh dill weed

1. With 2½-inch scalloped round cookie cutter, cut 24 rounds from cheese slices. With 1¾-inch round cutter, cut 24 rounds from ham slices (4 rounds can be cut from each ham slice).

2. Spoon about ½ teaspoon spreadable cheese on center of each bread slice. Place 1 cheese slice on spreadable cheese on each bread slice; press down gently. Place 1 ham slice on each cheese slice.

3. With 1¾-inch round cutter, cut small half-circle from top edge through ham, cheese and bread to form neck of bib (see photo). Repeat to make remaining bibs.

4. To make tie for each bib, cut each chive in half. Tie 2 chive halves together with knot in center to make X shape. Tuck remaining 2 chive ends under cheese slice on either side of cutout. Pipe spreadable cheese to form small design on bibs; garnish with dill weed.

1 Appetizer: Calories 90; Total Fat 6g (Saturated Fat 3.5g, Trans Fat 0g); Cholesterol 20mg; Sodium 190mg; Total Carbohydrate 4g (Dietary Fiber 0g); Protein 5g **Exchanges:** ½ Starch, ½ High-Fat Meat **Carbohydrate Choices:** 0

Tip For a meatless variation, use a variety of colored cheeses and vegetables such as zucchini slices, leaf lettuce and tomato slices.

Hummus and Cucumber Bites

Prep Time: 15 Minutes • **Start to Finish:** 15 Minutes • Makes 16 appetizers

2 pita (pocket) breads (6-inch)

⅔ Cup roasted red pepper hummus (from 7-oz container)

⅓ English (seedless) cucumber (about 4 inches)

½ teaspoon smoked Spanish paprika

16 sprigs fresh dill weed

1 Cut each pita bread into 8 wedges. Spread about 1 teaspoon hummus on each wedge.

2 Score cucumber peel lengthwise with tines of fork. Cut cucumber in half lengthwise. Cut each half crosswise into 16 thin slices. Place 2 half-slices cucumber on hummus on each wedge.

3 Sprinkle with paprika. Garnish with dill weed.

1 Appetizer: Calories 40; Total Fat 1g (Saturated Fat 0g, Trans Fat 0g); Cholesterol 0mg; Sodium 70mg; Total Carbohydrate 6g (Dietary Fiber 0g); Protein 1g **Exchanges:** ½ Starch **Carbohydrate Choices:** ½

Tip Smoked Spanish paprika has a smoky, spicy flavor, but you can use regular paprika instead.

Savory Bites

Roasted Red Bell Pepper and Goat Cheese Bites

Prep Time: 30 Minutes • **Start to Finish:** 40 Minutes • Makes 32 appetizers

1 box refrigerated pie crusts, softened as directed on box

1 container (5 oz) goat cheese

⅔ cup roasted red bell peppers (from 15-oz jar), drained, patted dry with paper towel and cut into ½-inch pieces

2½ teaspoons finely chopped fresh oregano leaves

2 teaspoons extra-virgin olive oil

¼ to ½ teaspoon garlic powder

Small fresh oregano leaves

1. Heat oven to 400°F. Line 2 large cookie sheets with cooking parchment paper. On floured work surface, unroll pie crust. Using 1¾-inch round cookie or canapé cutter, cut out 32 rounds; place about ½ inch apart on cookie sheets.

2. Spread about 1 teaspoon goat cheese on each dough round. Bake 10 to 12 minutes or until edges are light golden brown.

3. Meanwhile, in medium bowl, stir together roasted peppers, finely chopped oregano, oil and garlic powder until well blended.

4. Immediately top each baked cheese-topped round with 1 teaspoon red pepper mixture; place on serving platter. Garnish each with oregano leaf. Serve warm or at room temperature.

1 Appetizer: Calories 40; Total Fat 3g (Saturated Fat 1.5g, Trans Fat 0g); Cholesterol 0mg; Sodium 45mg; Total Carbohydrate 3g (Dietary Fiber 0g); Protein 1g **Exchanges:** 1 Fat **Carbohydrate Choices:** 0

Tip Look for cooking parchment paper with the other paper products at the supermarket. It's great for making cookies and other items — clean up is extra easy!

Mango-Pepper Salsa Crostini

Prep Time: 30 Minutes • **Start to Finish:** 1 Hour 30 Minutes • Makes 32 crostini

- ½ medium mango, pitted, peeled and diced (½ cup)
- 1 medium green onion, thinly sliced (1 tablespoon)
- ¼ cup diced red bell pepper
- 2 tablespoons chopped fresh cilantro
- ¼ jalapeño chile, seeded, finely chopped
- 2 tablespoons lime juice
- 1 container (8 oz) pineapple–cream cheese spread
- 32 thin slices baguette French bread

1. In medium glass or plastic bowl, mix all ingredients except cream cheese and bread. Cover; refrigerate 1 hour to blend flavors.

2. Spread cream cheese on baguette slices. Spoon about 1 teaspoon salsa over cream cheese, using slotted spoon.

1 Crostini: Calories 40; Total Fat 2g (Saturated Fat 1.5g, Trans Fat 0g); Cholesterol 5mg; Sodium 80mg; Total Carbohydrate 4g (Dietary Fiber 0g); Protein 1g **Exchanges:** ½ Starch **Carbohydrate Choices:** 0

Tip Make the fruit salsa a day ahead of time and refrigerate it.

Savory Bites

Tomato-Artichoke Bruschetta with Feta

Prep Time: 20 Minutes • **Start to Finish:** 20 Minutes • Makes 24 bruschetta

1 can (14.5 oz) fire-roasted diced tomatoes, drained

½ cup drained coarsely chopped artichoke hearts (from 14-oz can), patted dry with paper towels

1½ teaspoons chopped fresh thyme leaves

1 tablespoon olive oil

1 teaspoon balsamic vinegar

⅛ teaspoon freshly ground black pepper

24 slices (½ inch thick) baguette (about 8 oz), toasted*

½ cup crumbled feta cheese (2 oz)

1 In medium bowl, mix tomatoes, artichokes, thyme, oil, vinegar and pepper.

2 Spoon tomato mixture onto toasted baguette slices. Top with feta cheese. Serve immediately.

*To toast baguette slices, heat oven to 425°F. On ungreased cookie sheet, place bread slices. Bake 4 to 5 minutes or until very light golden brown.

1 Bruschetta: Calories 45; Total Fat 1.5g (Saturated Fat 0g, Trans Fat 0g); Cholesterol 0mg; Sodium 120mg; Total Carbohydrate 7g (Dietary Fiber 0g); Protein 1g **Exchanges:** ½ Starch **Carbohydrate Choices:** ½

Tip   Keep a pair of scissors in your kitchen for a quick snip of herbs. You can snip the thyme leaves quickly in a small bowl or measuring cup instead of chopping them with a knife.

Fresh Mozzarella in Tomato Cups

Prep Time: 15 Minutes • **Start to Finish:** 15 Minutes • Makes 12 appetizers

12 large cherry tomatoes
2 oz fresh mozzarella cheese, cut into ½-inch cubes
¼ cup Italian dressing
12 small basil leaves

1. Cut top off each cherry tomato. With melon baller or measuring spoon, scoop out seeds from each tomato, leaving enough for a firm shell. If necessary, cut small slice from bottom so tomato stands upright. Place tomatoes on serving plate or tray.

2. In small bowl, toss cheese and dressing. Place 1 cheese cube in each tomato; top each with basil leaf.

1 Appetizer: Calories 35; Total Fat 2.5g (Saturated Fat 0.5g, Trans Fat 0g); Cholesterol 0mg; Sodium 115mg; Total Carbohydrate 2g (Dietary Fiber 0g); Protein 1g **Exchanges:** ½ Fat **Carbohydrate Choices:** 0

Tip Fresh mozzarella is made with whole milk, is white and has a delicate, sweet, milky flavor. This soft cheese is packed in water or whey and is often formed into balls or slices.

Festive Fillo Crab Cups

Prep Time: 15 Minutes • **Start to Finish:** 15 Minutes • Makes 30 appetizers

2 cans (6 oz each) lump crabmeat, drained, flaked

¼ cup mayonnaise or salad dressing

¼ cup sour cream

3 tablespoons finely chopped celery

2 tablespoons finely chopped fresh chives

1 tablespoon finely chopped fresh dill weed

1 teaspoon lemon juice

½ teaspoon grated lemon peel

¼ teaspoon salt

½ teaspoon Worcestershire sauce

¼ teaspoon red pepper sauce

2 packages (2.1 oz each) frozen mini fillo shells (15 shells each)

Additional fresh dill weed sprigs, if desired

Fresh lemon slices, cut into quarters, if desired

1 In medium bowl, stir together all ingredients except fillo shells, additional dill weed sprigs and lemon slices until well mixed. Cover; refrigerate until ready to serve.

2 Spoon about 1 rounded tablespoon crab mixture into each fillo shell. Garnish each with dill weed sprig and lemon slices. Serve immediately.

1 Appetizer: Calories 45; Total Fat 3g (Saturated Fat 0g, Trans Fat 0g); Cholesterol 10mg; Sodium 75mg; Total Carbohydrate 2g (Dietary Fiber 0g); Protein 2g **Exchanges:** ½ High-Fat Meat **Carbohydrate Choices:** 0

Tip The filling can be made and refrigerated up to 8 hours ahead, then place in fillo shells just before serving.

Petite Treats

Baby Block Cereal Bars

Prep Time: 40 Minutes • **Start to Finish:** 1 Hour 40 Minutes • Makes 9 bars

¼ cup butter or margarine
1 bag (10½ oz) miniature marshmallows (5½ cups)
3 cups Cheerios® cereal
3 cups Kix® cereal
1 cup salted peanuts
Decorating icing (any colors)

1. Spray bottom and sides of 9-inch square pan with cooking spray. In large microwavable bowl, microwave butter uncovered on High about 45 seconds or until melted.

2. Add marshmallows; toss until coated. Microwave uncovered on High about 1 minute 30 seconds, stirring after 45 seconds, until mixture can be stirred smooth.

3. Immediately add cereals and peanuts; stir until evenly coated. Press firmly into pan. Cool about 1 hour or until firm. For bars, cut into 3 rows by 3 rows. Decorate as desired, using decorating icing. Store loosely covered.

1 Bar: Calories 410; Total Fat 18g (Saturated Fat 4.5g, Trans Fat 0g); Cholesterol 15mg; Sodium 330mg; Total Carbohydrate 57g (Dietary Fiber 3g); Protein 6g **Exchanges:** 2 Starch, 2 Other Carbohydrate, 3 Fat **Carbohydrate Choices:** 4

Tip For fun, use colored miniature marshmallows.

Lemon Linzer Bars

Prep Time: 20 Minutes • **Start to Finish:** 5 Hours 15 Minutes • Makes 24 bars

Cookie Base

- 1 pouch (1 lb 1.5 oz) Betty Crocker® sugar cookie mix
- ⅓ cup butter or margarine, softened
- 2 oz cream cheese, softened
- 4½ teaspoons frozen (thawed) lemonade concentrate
- ¾ teaspoon almond extract
- 1 egg

Filling

- ⅔ cup seedless raspberry jam
- 1 package (8 oz) cream cheese, softened
- ½ cup lemon curd (from 10- to 12-oz jar)
- 2 cups frozen (thawed) whipped topping or 2 cups sweetened whipped cream

Topping

- ⅓ cup sliced almonds, toasted*
- 24 fresh or frozen (thawed and drained) raspberries

1. Heat oven to 350°F. Spray bottom and sides of 13 x 9-inch pan with cooking spray.

2. In large bowl, stir all cookie base ingredients until soft dough forms. Spread dough in bottom of pan.

3. Bake 20 to 23 minutes or until golden brown. Cool completely, about 30 minutes.

4. Spread raspberry jam over cooled base. In large bowl, beat cream cheese and lemon curd with electric mixer on medium speed until smooth. Fold in whipped topping. Drop lemon mixture by teaspoonfuls over jam layer; spread gently and evenly over jam.

5. Sprinkle almonds over top. Refrigerate at least 4 hours or overnight.

6. For bars, cut into 6 rows by 4 rows. To serve, top each bar with 1 raspberry, gently pressing into lemon mixture. Store covered in refrigerator.

*To toast almonds, bake in ungreased shallow pan in 350°F oven about 10 minutes, stirring occasionally, until golden brown.

1 Bar: Calories 230; Total Fat 11g (Saturated Fat 6g, Trans Fat 1g); Cholesterol 35mg; Sodium 115mg; Total Carbohydrate 30g (Dietary Fiber 0g); Protein 2g **Exchanges:** 2 Other Carbohydrate, ½ High-Fat Meat, 1½ Fat **Carbohydrate Choices:** 2

Tip Lemon curd is a lovely, thick not-too-sweet product that you will find next to the jams and jellies at the grocery store.

Almond Petits Fours

Prep Time: 1 Hour 50 Minutes • **Start to Finish:** 1 Hour 50 Minutes • Makes 58 petits fours

Cake
1 box Betty Crocker SuperMoist® white cake mix

Water, vegetable oil and egg whites called for on cake mix box

1 teaspoon almond extract

Glaze
1 bag (2 lb) powdered sugar

½ cup water

½ cup corn syrup

2 teaspoons almond extract

1 to 3 teaspoons hot water

Decoration
Assorted colors decorating icing (in 4.25-oz tubes)

Fresh edible flowers or purchased candy flowers

1. Heat oven to 350°F (325°F for dark or nonstick pans). Spray bottoms only of 58 mini muffin cups with baking spray with flour.

2. Make cake batter as directed on box, adding 1 teaspoon almond extract with the water. Divide batter evenly among muffin cups, filling each about half full. (If using one pan, refrigerate remaining batter until ready to bake; cool pan before reusing.)

3. Bake 10 to 15 minutes or until toothpick inserted in center comes out clean. Cool 5 minutes; remove from pan to cooling rack. Cool completely, about 30 minutes.

4. Place cooling rack on cookie sheet or waxed paper to catch glaze drips. In 3-quart saucepan, stir powdered sugar, ½ cup water, the corn syrup and 2 teaspoons almond extract. Heat over low heat, stirring frequently, until sugar is dissolved; remove from heat. Stir in hot water, 1 teaspoon at a time, until glaze is pourable. Turn each cake top side down on cooling rack. Pour about 1 tablespoon glaze over each cake, letting glaze coat the sides. Let stand 15 minutes.

5. With decorating icing, pipe designs on cakes; or garnish cakes with flowers just before serving. Store loosely covered.

1 Petit Four: Calories 110; Total Fat 1.5g (Saturated Fat 0g, Trans Fat 0g); Cholesterol 0mg; Sodium 60mg; Total Carbohydrate 24g (Dietary Fiber 0g); Protein 0g **Exchanges:** ½ Starch, 1 Other Carbohydrate **Carbohydrate Choices:** 1½

Tip You can make the cupcakes up to 2 weeks earlier and freeze, but wait to add the glaze until shortly before you serve them.

Mini Almond-Butter Tea Cakes

Prep Time: 35 Minutes • **Start to Finish:** 2 Hours • Makes 24 tea cakes

½ cup butter (do not use margarine)
½ cup slivered almonds
1 cup powdered sugar
½ cup Gold Medal® all-purpose flour
¼ teaspoon salt
1 teaspoon vanilla
¼ teaspoon almond extract
4 egg whites
½ cup sliced almonds
2 teaspoons white decorator sugar crystals

1 Heat oven to 375°F. Line 8-inch square pan with foil; spray foil with cooking spray. In 2-quart saucepan, heat butter over medium-high heat about 5 minutes, stirring frequently, until a rich hazelnut-brown color. Remove from heat; cool 5 minutes.

2 Meanwhile, in food processor, process slivered almonds until finely ground. In large bowl, stir together ground almonds, powdered sugar, flour and salt. Add vanilla, almond extract and egg whites; beat about 1 minute or until blended.

3 On medium speed, beat in browned butter until smooth, about 1 minute. Pour batter into pan. Sprinkle sliced almonds evenly over batter; sprinkle sugar crystals evenly over almonds.

4 Bake 20 to 25 minutes or until golden brown. Cool completely, about 1 hour. Using foil, lift cake from pan; remove foil from cake. Cut into 6 rows by 4 rows.

1 Tea Cake: Calories 130; Total Fat 8g (Saturated Fat 3.5g, Trans Fat 0g); Cholesterol 15mg; Sodium 85mg; Total Carbohydrate 11g (Dietary Fiber 0g); Protein 2g **Exchanges:** 1 Other Carbohydrate, 1½ Fat **Carbohydrate Choices:** 1

Tip For a deeper almond flavor, toast the almonds before grinding them. Place them in a single layer on a cookie sheet, then bake in a 375°F oven 5 to 8 minutes or until they're golden brown.

Salted Caramel Turtle Triangles

Prep Time: 20 Minutes • **Start to Finish:** 1 Hour 30 Minutes • Makes 48 triangles

Cookie Base

- 1 pouch (1 lb 1.5 oz) Betty Crocker double chocolate chunk cookie mix
- ¼ cup butter or margarine, melted
- 2 tablespoons water
- 1 egg
- ⅔ cup pecans, coarsely chopped

Topping

- 4 tablespoons butter
- 1 bag (14 oz) caramels, approximately 50 caramels
- ¼ cup whipping cream
- ½ teaspoon vanilla
- ⅛ teaspoon coarse (kosher or sea) salt, plus additional ½ teaspoon for top of bars

1. Heat oven to 350°F. Spray 9 x 13-inch pan with cooking spray.

2. In medium bowl, stir together cookie mix, butter, water and egg until soft dough forms. Press into pan. Sprinkle with ⅓ cup of the pecans. Bake 11 to 15 minutes or until set in center and edges just begin to pull away from sides of pan. Set aside to cool.

3. Meanwhile, in medium saucepan, melt butter, caramels and cream over medium-low heat, stirring frequently until mixture is smooth. Remove from heat. Stir in vanilla and ⅛ teaspoon salt.

4. Spread caramel evenly over cookie base. Sprinkle with remaining pecans. Cool completely. Sprinkle top of caramel with additional salt just before serving. Cut into 4 rows by 6 rows, and cut each square diagonally into triangles. Store in refrigerator; bring to room temperature before serving.

1 Triangle: Calories 110; Total Fat 5g (Saturated Fat 2.5g, Trans Fat 0g); Cholesterol 15mg; Sodium 110mg; Total Carbohydrate 15g (Dietary Fiber 0g); Protein 1g **Exchanges:** 1 Other Carbohydrate, 1 Fat **Carbohydrate Choices:** 1

Tip These decadent caramel-topped bars will be a favorite at your shower. Show them off on a pretty plate surrounded with favorite fresh fruit.

Petite Treats

Cherry-Topped Chocolate Tassies

Prep Time: 25 Minutes • **Start to Finish:** 1 Hour 10 Minutes • Makes 2 dozen cookies

½ cup butter, softened
1 package (3 oz) cream cheese, softened
1 cup Gold Medal all-purpose flour
⅛ teaspoon salt
1 cup miniature semisweet chocolate chips
24 large maraschino cherries, drained

1 Heat oven to 350°F. Spray 24 mini muffin cups with cooking spray.

2 In medium bowl, beat butter and cream cheese with electric mixer on medium speed until well mixed. On low speed, beat in flour and salt until dough forms.

3 Shape dough into 24 (1¼-inch) balls. Press 1 ball in bottom and up side of each muffin cup. Fill each cup with about 2 teaspoons chocolate chips. Top each with 1 cherry.

4 Bake 13 to 16 minutes or until edges of cups are golden brown. Cool 10 minutes. Remove from pan to cooling racks; cool completely, about 20 minutes.

1 Cookie: Calories 110; Total Fat 7g (Saturated Fat 4.5g, Trans Fat 0g); Cholesterol 15mg; Sodium 50mg; Total Carbohydrate 10g (Dietary Fiber 0g); Protein 1g **Exchanges:** ½ Other Carbohydrate, 1½ Fat **Carbohydrate Choices:** ½

Tip While cookies are still hot, sprinkle cookie edges with powdered sugar or red decorator sugar.

Luscious Chocolate Truffles

Prep Time: 20 Minutes • **Start to Finish:** 1 Hour 15 Minutes • Makes 15 truffles

1 bag (12 oz) semisweet chocolate chips (2 cups)

2 tablespoons butter or margarine

¼ cup whipping cream

2 tablespoons liqueur (almond, cherry, coffee, hazelnut, Irish cream, orange, raspberry, etc.), if desired

1 tablespoon shortening

Finely chopped nuts, if desired

Finely chopped dried apricots, if desired

White chocolate baking bar, chopped, if desired

1 Line cookie sheet with foil or cooking parchment paper. In 2-quart saucepan, melt 1 cup of the chocolate chips over low heat, stirring constantly; remove from heat. Stir in butter. Stir in whipping cream and liqueur. Refrigerate 10 to 15 minutes, stirring frequently, just until thick enough to hold a shape.

2 Drop mixture by teaspoonfuls onto cookie sheet. Shape into balls. (If mixture is too sticky, refrigerate until firm enough to shape.) Freeze 30 minutes.

3 In 1-quart saucepan, heat shortening and remaining 1 cup chocolate chips over low heat, stirring constantly, until chocolate is melted and mixture is smooth; remove from heat. Dip truffles, one at a time, into chocolate, placing each truffle on fork and dipping into chocolate to coat. Lift fork from chocolate and allow excess chocolate to drip off. Return to cookie sheet. Immediately sprinkle nuts and apricots over some of the truffles. Reheat chocolate dipping mixture, if necessary. Refrigerate truffles about 10 minutes or until coating is set.

4 In 1-quart saucepan, heat baking bar over low heat, stirring constantly, until melted. Drizzle over some of the truffles. Refrigerate just until set. Store in tightly covered container in refrigerator. Remove truffles from refrigerator about 30 minutes before serving; serve at room temperature.

1 Truffle: Calories 160; Total Fat 10g (Saturated Fat 6g, Trans Fat 0g); Cholesterol 10mg; Sodium 15mg; Total Carbohydrate 14g (Dietary Fiber 1g); Protein 1g **Exchanges:** 1 Other Carbohydrate, 2 Fat **Carbohydrate Choices:** 1

Tip You can make these delightful truffles up to a week ahead — just take them out of the refrigerator about half an hour before serving for better flavor and texture.

Celebratory Cakes

Baby's Booties

Prep Time: 25 Minutes • **Start to Finish:** 1 Hour 50 Minutes • Makes 16 booties (made from 24 cupcakes)

1 box Betty Crocker SuperMoist cake mix (any flavor)

Water, vegetable oil and eggs called for on cake mix box

2 containers (12- or 16-oz each) Betty Crocker Rich & Creamy or Whipped vanilla frosting

Miniature marshmallows

Large gumdrops

1 Heat oven to 350°F (325°F for dark or nonstick pans). Place paper baking cup in each of 24 regular-size muffin cups. Make and bake cake mix as directed on box for 24 cupcakes. Cool 10 minutes; remove from pans to cooling rack. Cool completely, about 30 minutes.

2 Remove paper baking cups. Place 2 cupcakes upside down on separate plates (1 cupcake on each plate). Cut small piece off side of a third cupcake to make a flat surface as shown in diagram 1. Cut third cupcake horizontally in half as shown in diagram 2. Place one half with cut side against cupcake on plate as shown in diagram 3. Place other half against second cupcake. Repeat with remaining cupcakes.

3 Frost cupcake booties, attaching toe piece to cupcake with frosting. Decorate with marshmallows and bow shapes cut from gumdrops rolled with a rolling pin. Store loosely covered.

1 Bootie (Cake and Frosting Only): Calories 400; Total Fat 16g (Saturated Fat 3.5g, Trans Fat 3.5g); Cholesterol 35mg; Sodium 300mg; Total Carbohydrate 62g (Dietary Fiber 0g); Protein 1g **Exchanges:** ½ Starch, 3½ Other Carbohydrate, 3 Fat **Carbohydrate Choices:** 4

Tip Create bootie colors of your choice by stirring drops of food color into frosting.

Cutting and Assembling Baby's Booties

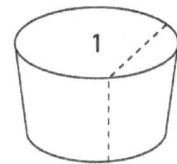

1. Cut piece off side of 1 cupcake.

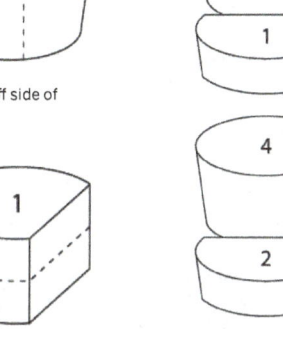

2. Cut cupcake horizontally in half.

3. Place halves with cut sides against 2 other cupcakes.

Baby Rattle Cupcakes

Prep Time: 45 Minutes • **Start to Finish:** 1 Hour 45 Minutes • Makes 24 cupcakes

- 1 box Betty Crocker SuperMoist cake mix (any flavor)
- Water, vegetable oil and eggs called for on cake mix box
- 1 container (1 lb) Betty Crocker Rich & Creamy vanilla or creamy white frosting
- Yellow and green decorating icings (from 4.25-oz tubes)
- Colored candy sprinkles, if desired
- 8 yards pastel satin or curling ribbon (¼ inch), if desired
- 24 paper lollipop sticks (4½ inch)
- 24 small gumdrops

1 Heat oven to 350°F (325°F for dark or nonstick pans). Place paper baking cup in each of 24 regular-size muffin cups. Make and bake cake mix as directed on box for 24 cupcakes. Cool 10 minutes; remove from pans to cooling rack. Cool completely, about 30 minutes.

2 Frost cupcakes with vanilla frosting. Pipe designs on cupcakes with yellow and green icings. Decorate as desired with candy sprinkles.

3 With toothpick, poke hole in side of each cupcake. Tie ribbon bow in center of each lollipop stick. Add gumdrop to one end of each stick. Insert other ends of sticks into sides of cupcakes, just below frosting, to form rattles. Store loosely covered.

1 Cupcake (Cake and Frosting Only): Calories 190; Total Fat 9g (Saturated Fat 2g, Trans Fat 1g); Cholesterol 25mg; Sodium 180mg; Total Carbohydrate 28g (Dietary Fiber 0g); Protein 1g **Exchanges:** ½ Starch, 1½ Other Carbohydrate, 1½ Fat **Carbohydrate Choices:** 2

Tip If you have only one pan and a recipe calls for more cupcakes than your pan will make, cover and refrigerate the rest of the batter while baking the first batch. Cool the pan about 15 minutes, then bake the rest of the batter, adding 1 to 2 minutes to the bake time.

Baby Face Cake

Prep Time: 40 Minutes • **Start to Finish:** 2 Hours 50 Minutes • Makes 16 servings

1 box Betty Crocker SuperMoist white cake mix

Water, vegetable oil and egg whites called for on cake mix box

½ teaspoon almond extract

1 tube red or blue gel food color (from 2.7-oz box)

1 container (12 oz) Betty Crocker Whipped fluffy white frosting

1 can (8.4 oz) pink or blue cupcake icing

1 can (8.4 oz) yellow cupcake icing

1 large marshmallow, cut in half

1. Heat oven to 350°F (325°F for dark or nonstick pans). Grease bottoms only of 2 (8-inch) round cake pans with shortening or cooking spray. Make cake batter as directed on box, adding almond extract and 4 drops red or blue food color with the water. Bake as directed on box for 8-inch rounds.

2. Cool 10 minutes. Run knife around sides of pans to loosen cakes; remove from pans to cooling rack. Cool completely, about 1 hour.

3. On serving plate, place 1 cake layer bottom side up. Spread with ½ cup white frosting. Top with second layer. Frost side and top of cake.

4. Pipe decorating icing around bottom and top of cake using border tip and pink or blue icing. Use yellow cupcake icing to make baby pacifier and hair. Use desired decorating icing to make face and hair bow. Place marshmallow half over yellow icing to complete baby pacifier. Store loosely covered at room temperature.

1 Serving (Frosted, Undecorated): Calories 150; Total Fat 6g (Saturated Fat 1.5g, Trans Fat 0g); Cholesterol 0mg; Sodium 210mg; Total Carbohydrate 23g (Dietary Fiber 0g); Protein 2g **Exchanges:** ½ Starch, 1 Other Carbohydrate, 1 Fat **Carbohydrate Choices:** 1½

Tip Since pacifiers come in so many colors, substitute a colored marshmallow for a white one.

Baby Buggy Cake

Prep Time: 50 Minutes • **Start to Finish:** 2 Hours 50 Minutes • Makes 12 servings

- 1 box Betty Crocker SuperMoist white cake mix
- Water, vegetable oil and egg whites called for on cake mix box
- ½ teaspoon almond extract
- Blue or red food color from 1 box (2.7 oz) gel food colors
- 1 container (12 oz) Betty Crocker Whipped fluffy white frosting
- 1 can (8.4 oz) blue or pink cupcake icing
- 1 can (6.4 oz) white decorating icing
- 1 colored plastic straw

1 Heat oven to 350°F (325°F for dark or nonstick pans). Grease and flour bottom only of 8-inch round cake pan. Place paper baking cup in each of 12 regular-size muffin cups.

2 Make cake batter as directed on box, adding almond extract and 2 drops blue or red food color with the water. Spread half of the batter in round pan; divide remaining batter evenly among muffin cups. Bake as directed on box for 8-inch round and cupcakes. Cool 10 minutes. Remove from pans to cooling rack. Cool completely, about 1 hour.

3 On serving platter, place cake layer bottom side up. Frost side and top of cake and 2 of the cupcakes with white frosting. (Frost remaining cupcakes, and serve on the side.)

4 To make baby buggy, pipe half of top side of cake with blue or pink cupcake icing, using basket-weave tip. For buggy hood, pipe one-quarter of top side of cake with blue or pink cupcake icing, using star tip. Pipe around edge with white decorating icing. Pipe white lines on buggy hood. Add baby face as desired.

5 To make buggy wheels, pipe blue or pink cupcake icing for spokes on each of 2 cupcakes and around edge of each cupcake. Place cupcakes at bottom of cake for wheels. Add straw for buggy handle. Store loosely covered at room temperature.

1 Serving: Calories 450; Total Fat 19g (Saturated Fat 4.5g, Trans Fat 2.5g); Cholesterol 0mg; Sodium 340mg; Total Carbohydrate 67g (Dietary Fiber 0g); Protein 2g **Exchanges:** 1 Starch, 3½ Other Carbohydrate, 3½ Fat **Carbohydrate Choices:** 4½

Tip If you'd prefer, use green or yellow cupcake icing instead.

Baby's Bib Cake

Prep Time: 30 Minutes • **Start to Finish:** 2 Hours 20 Minutes • Makes 16 servings

1 box Betty Crocker SuperMoist cake mix (any flavor)

Water, vegetable oil and eggs called for on cake mix box

2 containers (1 lb each) Betty Crocker Rich & Creamy vanilla frosting

Red food color

Blue food color

1. Heat oven to 350°F (325°F for dark or nonstick pans). Make, bake and cool cake as directed on box for 2 (8- or 9-inch) rounds.

2. Reserve 1 cup frosting for decorating. Place 1 cake layer, rounded side down, on serving plate. Spread with about ⅓ cup frosting. Place other layer, rounded side up, on top. Frost side and top of cake with remaining frosting. Make vertical lines on side of cake with decorating comb or tines of fork if desired.

3. Tint ⅔ cup of the reserved frosting pink with 1 or 2 drops red food color. Place pink frosting in decorating bag with small writing tip #2. Pipe 2 circles around outer top edge of cake, about 1 inch apart, leaving 3-inch opening at top. Make loop design within circles.

4. Tint remaining ⅓ cup frosting blue with 1 or 2 drops blue food color. Place blue frosting in decorating bag with writing tip #5. Pipe outer border of bib. Pipe inner opening of bib about 3 inches in diameter; join circles with tie at top. Make small bows on bib and write desired message in bib opening. Pipe dots between bows with remaining pink frosting if desired. Store loosely covered.

1 Serving: Calories 400; Total Fat 17g (Saturated Fat 3.5g, Trans Fat 3.5g); Cholesterol 40mg; Sodium 320mg; Total Carbohydrate 60g (Dietary Fiber 0g); Protein 1g **Exchanges:** ½ Starch, 3½ Other Carbohydrate, 3½ Fat **Carbohydrate Choices:** 4

Tip If you don't have decorating bags and tips to pipe the frosting, place the frosting in a resealable food-storage plastic bag, and snip off a small corner to make a writing tip.

Baby Block Cake

Prep Time: 40 Minutes • **Start to Finish:** 2 Hours 25 Minutes • Makes 12 servings

Cake

1 box Betty Crocker SuperMoist white cake mix

Water, vegetable oil and egg whites called for on cake mix box

½ teaspoon almond extract

1 box (2.7 oz) gel food colors

Frosting and Decorations

1 container (12 oz) Betty Crocker Whipped fluffy white frosting

Decorating icing (any colors)

Star-shaped candy sprinkles

1 Heat oven to 350°F (325°F for dark or nonstick pans). Grease or spray bottoms only of 2 (8-inch) square pans. Make cake batter as directed on box, adding almond extract with the water. Place half of batter in separate bowl. Stir 2 drops blue food color into batter in 1 bowl; stir 2 drops red food color into remaining batter. Pour 1 color batter into each pan.

2 Bake 25 to 31 minutes or until toothpick inserted in center comes out clean. Cool 10 minutes. Run knife around pans to loosen cakes; remove from pans to cooling racks. Cool completely, about 1 hour.

3 Place 1 cake layer, bottom side up, on serving plate. Spread with ½ cup frosting. Top with second cake layer, bottom side down. Frost side and top of cake. Using decorating icing, decorate cake as desired to look like baby block. Sprinkle top of cake with candy sprinkles. Store loosely covered.

1 Serving: Calories 330; Total Fat 14g (Saturated Fat 3.5g, Trans Fat 2g); Cholesterol 0mg; Sodium 310mg; Total Carbohydrate 48g (Dietary Fiber 0g); Protein 2g **Exchanges:** 1 Starch, 2 Other Carbohydrate, 2½ Fat **Carbohydrate Choices:** 3

Tip If you'd prefer, use green and yellow food colors, or make both of the cakes the same color. You choose!

Metric Conversion Guide

Volume

U.S. Units	Canadian Metric	Australian Metric
¼ teaspoon	1 mL	1 ml
½ teaspoon	2 mL	2 ml
1 teaspoon	5 mL	5 ml
1 tablespoon	15 mL	20 ml
¼ cup	50 mL	60 ml
⅓ cup	75 mL	80 ml
½ cup	125 mL	125 ml
⅔ cup	150 mL	170 ml
¾ cup	175 mL	190 ml
1 cup	250 mL	250 ml
1 quart	1 liter	1 liter
1½ quarts	1.5 liters	1.5 liters
2 quarts	2 liters	2 liters
2½ quarts	2.5 liters	2.5 liters
3 quarts	3 liters	3 liters
4 quarts	4 liters	4 liters

Weight

U.S. Units	Canadian Metric	Australian Metric
1 ounce	30 grams	30 grams
2 ounces	55 grams	60 grams
3 ounces	85 grams	90 grams
4 ounces (¼ pound)	115 grams	125 grams
8 ounces (½ pound)	225 grams	225 grams
16 ounces (1 pound)	455 grams	500 grams
1 pound	455 grams	0.5 kilogram

Note: The recipes in this cookbook have not been developed or tested using metric measures. When converting recipes to metric, some variations in quality may be noted.

Measurements

Inches	Centimeters
1	2.5
2	5.0
3	7.5
4	10.0
5	12.5
6	15.0
7	17.5
8	20.5
9	23.0
10	25.5
11	28.0
12	30.5
13	33.0

Temperatures

Fahrenheit	Celsius
32°	0°
212°	100°
250°	120°
275°	140°
300°	150°
325°	160°
350°	180°
375°	190°
400°	200°
425°	220°
450°	230°
475°	240°
500°	260°

Recipe Testing and Calculating Nutrition Information

Recipe Testing:

- Large eggs and 2% milk were used unless otherwise indicated.
- Fat-free, low-fat, low-sodium or lite products were not used unless indicated.
- No nonstick cookware and bakeware were used unless otherwise indicated. No dark-colored, black or insulated bakeware was used.
- When a pan is specified, a metal pan was used; a baking dish or pie plate means ovenproof glass was used.
- An electric hand mixer was used for mixing only when mixer speeds are specified.

Calculating Nutrition:

- The first ingredient was used wherever a choice is given, such as ⅓ cup sour cream or plain yogurt.
- The first amount was used wherever a range is given, such as 3- to 3½-pound whole chicken.
- The first serving number was used wherever a range is given, such as 4 to 6 servings.
- "If desired" ingredients were not included.
- Only the amount of a marinade or frying oil that is absorbed was included.

America's most trusted cookbook is better than ever!

- 1,100 all-new photos, including hundreds of step-by-step images
- More than 1,500 recipes, with hundreds of inspiring variations and creative "mini" recipes for easy cooking ideas
- Brand-new features
- Gorgeous new design

Get the best edition of the *Betty Crocker Cookbook* today!

www.ingramcontent.com/pod-product-compliance
Lightning Source LLC
Chambersburg PA
CBHW071417290426
44108CB00014B/1867